Economic and Social Commission for Asia and the Pacific

Sexually Abused and Sexually Exploited Children and Youth in South Asia: A Qualitative Assessment of their Health Needs and Available Services

UNITED NATIONS

New York, 1999

ST/ESCAP/2038

UNITED NATIONS PUBLICATION
Sales No. E.00.II.F.47
Copyright © United Nations 2000
ISBN: 92-1-119996-4

Foreword

Sexual abuse and sexual exploitation of children and youth are issues that urgently need to be addressed in South Asia. In addition to thriving cross-border trafficking networks, which lure or force children into prostitution, young people are increasingly entering commercial sex work "willingly", unaware of the conditions in which they will work or what the mental and physical consequences will be. In addition, socio-economic and cultural factors make young people susceptible to sexual exploitation, such as lack of education, family breakdown, lack of economic opportunities, traditional beliefs and practices and poverty. Children and youth in the region are also at risk of sexual abuse, usually by someone whom they know and trust. Young victims of sexual abuse and sexual exploitation are at high risk of contracting sexually transmitted diseases (STDs), including HIV/AIDS, as well as developing mental and behavioural problems. These children and youth need urgent and skilled social, psychological and medical services. Hence, in addition to critical prevention programmes, specialized services are crucial in order to facilitate recovery.

The prevention of sexual abuse and sexual exploitation of children and youth is a high priority for the United Nations. The Universal Declaration of Human Rights as well as the International Covenant on Economic, Social and Cultural Rights call for the protection of children's human rights. Furthermore, international instruments, such as the Convention on the Rights of the Child (CRC) and the ILO Convention 182 concerning the Prohibition and Immediate Action for the Elimination of the Worst Forms of Child Labour, call on states to protect children from sexual exploitation.

In addition to the above-mentioned instruments, the World Congress Against Commercial Sexual Exploitation of Children (Stockholm, 1996) galvanized the attention of the international community to the plight of sexually exploited children and the need for a global partnership to end the commercial sexual exploitation of children.

Against the above background, the member governments of ESCAP, in April 1997, unanimously adopted Resolution 53/4 entitled "Elimination of sexual abuse and exploitation of children and youth in Asia and the Pacific". This resolution signaled the firm resolve of the governments of the Asia-Pacific region to tackle the many challenges of preventing and combating sexual abuse and sexual exploitation among its young citizens

The current ESCAP programme is in direct response to resolution 53/4 and the needs of children and youth in the region, with a focus on strengthening the human resources development (HRD) capabilities of social service and health personnel to assist young victims and potential victims of sexual abuse and sexual exploitation. It is hoped that this present report on South Asia will promote awareness among governments, NGOs, and communities at large, of the situation facing today's sexually abused and sexually exploited children and youth. It remains the challenge of all sectors of society to formulate effective responses in order to bring about positive change and the realization of all young people's human rights.

I would like to express our gratitude to the Government of Japan for financing ESCAP's project on "Elimination of sexual abuse and sexual exploitation of children and youth in South Asia", as well as funding the present study.

Adrianus Mooy
Executive Secretary
Economic and Social Commission
for Asia and the Pacific

Abbreviations

AIDS	acquired immune deficiency syndrome
ASK	Ain O Salish Kendro
CWIN	Child Workers in Nepal
HIV	human immunodeficiency virus
NGO	non-governmental organization
Sida	Swedish International Development Cooperation Agency
STD	sexually transmitted disease
UNFPA	United Nations Population Fund
UNDCP	United Nations International Drug Control Programme
UNICEF	United Nations Children's Fund
WCD	Department of Women and Child Development

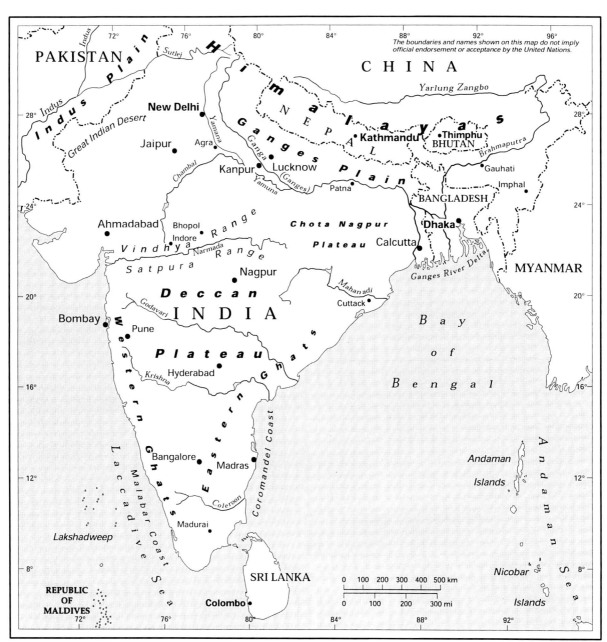

PAKISTAN

Indus

Indus Plain

Indus

Sutlej

72°   76°   80°   84°   88°   92°   96°

The boundaries and names shown on this map do not imply
official endorsement or acceptance by the United Nations.

28°

C H I N A

Yarlung Zangbo

Himalayas

New Delhi

Yamuna

N E P A L

28°

Jaipur

Agra

Ganga

Kathmandu

•**Thimphu**
BHUTAN

Brahmaputra

Great Indian Desert

Kanpur   Lucknow

Ganges Plain

Chambal

Yamuna

Ganga (Ganges)

Patna

BANGLADESH

• Gauhati

• Imphal

24°

24°

Ahmadabad

Bhopol

Indore

Vindhya

Range

Chota Nagpur

Dhaka

Narmada   *Range*

Plateau

Calcutta

Satpura

Nagpur

Mahanadi

Ganges River Delta

MYANMAR

20°

Deccan

Cuttack

20°

Bombay

Godavari

I N D I A

B a y

Pune

Plateau

Western Ghats

Krishna

Hyderabad

o f

16°

Eastern Ghats

B e n g a l

16°

Coromandel Coast

A n d a m a n

Bangalore

Madras

Andaman
Islands

12°

Laccadive Sea

Malabar Coast

Coleroon

Madurai

S e a

12°

Lakshadweep

Nicobar

8°

REPUBLIC
OF
MALDIVES

72°

SRI LANKA

Colombo •

Islands

8°

0   100 200 300 400 500 km

0   100   200   300 mi

76°   80°   84°   88°   92°

MAP NO. 3665   UNITED NATIONS
JANUARY 1992

Contents

Contents *(continued)*

Preface

The United Nations Economic and Social Commission for Asia and the Pacific (ESCAP), at its fifty-third session on 30 April 1997, adopted Resolution 53/4 on "Elimination of sexual abuse and sexual exploitation of children and youth in Asia and the Pacific". The adoption of this resolution represented a breakthrough in terms of reaching a regional consensus on action to address the growing problem of sexual abuse and exploitation of children and youth in the Asia-Pacific region.

With the above mandate, the Human Resources Development Section of the Social Development Division of ESCAP established a regional programme to eliminate sexual abuse and sexual exploitation of children and youth. The programme was developed in response to both the ESCAP resolution as well as to the call from the World Congress against Commercial Sexual Exploitation of Children (Stockholm, August 1996) to intensify international and regional efforts to eliminate the sexual exploitation of children.

The 12 participating countries in the regional programme are: Bangladesh, Cambodia, China (Yunnan Province), India, Lao People's Democratic Republic, Myanmar, Nepal, Pakistan, the Philippines, Sri Lanka, Thailand and Viet Nam.

The regional programme is supported by a consortium of donors comprising the Swedish International Development Cooperation Agency (Sida), the Governments of Australia and Japan, the United Nations International Drug Control Programme (UNDCP), the United Nations Population Fund (UNFPA), and UNAIDS.

The purpose of the ESCAP regional programme is to strengthen the human resources development capabilities of social service and health personnel who come into contact with young victims of sexual abuse and sexual exploitation. The programme aims to enhance the skills and knowledge of social and health service providers to more effectively assist young victims and potential victims of sexual abuse and exploitation to: (a) be reintegrated into communities and families; (b) have access to relevant health and social services; and (c) develop skills for alternative means of livelihood.

Victims and potential victims of sexual abuse and sexual exploitation are in great need of health and social services as well as psychological and career counselling. Social development personnel play a critical role in the prevention of abuse and exploitation as well as in the recovery of the victims and their reintegration into society. They are in direct contact with the target group through the provision of services, such as education and health care and are, therefore, in a position to address the specific needs of the target group.

The present subregional report on South Asia is one of many outcomes of the regional programme. The subregional report provides a synthesis of the situation relating to child sexual exploitation and child sexual abuse in five countries of South Asia, namely, Bangladesh, India, Nepal, Pakistan and Sri Lanka. It is based on the national reports prepared and submitted by each country's national research team, comprising representatives of government agencies, non-governmental organizations and/or academic institutions.

This report was prepared by ESCAP in collaboration with Mr. Hervé Berger, Former Deputy Secretary-General of Amnesty International and Executive Director of ECPAT International, during his tenure as a Consultant with ESCAP.

The preparation of the present subregional report has been financed by the Government of Japan, as one of many activities under the multi-year project titled "Elimination of sexual abuse and exploitation of youth through human resources development".

Chapter I

Introduction

A. OBJECTIVES OF THIS STUDY

Three objectives have been identified for this study, along with three distinct desired outputs. While the authors of the national studies attempted, to the best of their ability, to meet these objectives, some had difficulty for reasons including the sensitive nature of the subject matter in their national context.

1. Objectives

(a) To collect and analyse existing information on the country context, child sexual abuse (rape and incest) and child sexual exploitation (trafficking, pornography and prostitution) in the participating countries;

(b) To identify common health (medical, psychological and social) problems and needs of sexually abused and exploited children;

(c) To explore the range of services available to sexually abused and exploited children and the capacities and potential of the different agencies to provide these services.

2. Desired outputs

(a) A study to promote awareness of the situation of sexually abused and exploited children, focusing on their comprehensive health needs and the services available to them. The study will also serve as the basis for the development of training materials for social service and health personnel working with this group of children as well as for the development of other inter-ventions;

(b) A directory with profiles of organizations providing social and health services to sexually abused and exploited children in the participating countries to be drawn up;

(c) A bibliography of published and unpublished materials on sexually abused and exploited children to be compiled.

B. Target population

The study focused on children and youth aged 18 and below who have been sexually abused and/or engaged in commercial sexual exploitation for the purpose of making a living for themselves or their families. *Child sexual abuse* is defined as contacts or interactions between a child and an older or more knowledgeable child or adult (stranger, sibling or person in a position of authority such as a parent or caretaker) when the child is being used as an object for the older child's or adult's sexual needs. These contacts or interactions are carried out against the child using force, trickery, bribes, threats or pressure. *Child sexual exploitation* is defined as the use of a child for sexual purposes in exchange for cash or in-kind favours between the customer, intermediary or agent and others who profit from the trade in children for these purposes (parent, family member, procurer, teacher etc). A second target group of the study were the providers of medical, psychological and/or social services to the children in the first target group.

C. Report organization

This synthesis report is organized in four chapters. The first chapter provides background to this study, its objectives, target population and methodology.

The second chapter provides a brief overview of the situation of sexual exploitation of children and child sexual abuse in the South Asian subregion.

The third chapter focuses on health-related findings. The first part of this chapter looks at the various health needs of sexually exploited and sexually abused children, dividing these needs into key areas. The second part gives an overview of the health service providers and the type of services that they supply.

The fourth chapter is also divided into two parts. The first part summarizes the main conclusions of the various national reports, giving an overview of the key findings that apply across the subregion. The second part provides an overview of the key recommendations that emerge from the national reports. These recommendations are also of interest at the subregional level.

Finally, the annex provides the reader with case studies of victims of sexual exploitation and of sexual abuse. The second part of the annex gives an overview of three service providers.

This report is intended only to provide a summary of the South Asian subregional situation. The national reports provide significantly more information about the situation in each country and should be referred to for a more in-depth view.

D. Methodology

ESCAP identified local organizations to undertake or to coordinate research in each participating country: Ain O Salish Kendro (ASK) in Bangladesh; the College of Social Work at Nirmala Niketan Institute in India; the Centre for Women/Children and Community Development in Nepal; the National Commission for Child Welfare and Development in Pakistan; and Protecting Environment and Children Everywhere in Sri Lanka. ESCAP then provided the national research teams with a suggested methodology based primarily on qualitative data collection.   This methodology was developed by the International Maternal Child Health Section of Uppsala University in Uppsala, Sweden. It used observation and semi-structured interviews reinforced by the snowball method in which respondents were asked to recommend other people to be interviewed. This method allowed interviewers to locate victims of sexual abuse and exploitation in a way that would not be possible through random sampling.   The snowballing method was not used in Pakistan, however, because it was not well suited to the cultural context there. The use of secondary data further strengthened the data collection in each country, especially in India.

A total of 467 sexually abused and sexually exploited children were interviewed as part of the primary data collection. For the interviews, a semi-structured interview procedure was used to probe the children's history; their entry into prostitution or their experience with sexual abuse; their health needs; and their assessment of the care they received. One exception was in Bangladesh where structured interviews were used. In Sri Lanka, case studies and observation of sexually abused and exploited children supplemented the data collected through interviews. The interviews were carried out with sensitivity to the children's feelings and their traumatic past.

Among the children who did not appear to have any major emotional problems and who seemed to have recovered from the emotional impact of sexual abuse or sexual exploitation, the inter-viewer sought permission from the child to take notes. For children who manifested emotional problems or appeared embarrassed or shy, the interview was conducted without note taking or the use of a tape recorder. The results of the interviews in such cases were recorded following the interview.

Additional cases were obtained via secondary data collection in interviews with institutions and non-governmental organizations (NGOs) where the children were found as well as with social workers, health service providers, clients, key informants and lawyers. Secondary data was also used in all studies to confirm what was already known about the subject matter. The sources for the data were mainly reports published by various institutions and researchers as well as newspapers and other readily available publications. Information collected by NGOs and the records of relevant NGOs and other institutions, such as law enforcement agencies, were also consulted.

Among care providers, a semi-structured interview procedure was used to collect data on the nature of services, capabilities and potential of care providers, and problems encountered in providing care to the target groups.

With the exception of ASK in Bangladesh, no efforts were made to collect quantitative data on the incidence of child sexual abuse and child sexual exploitation in the countries covered in this report.

Limitations

Cultural taboos and the illegality of sexual abuse, prostitution and sexual exploitation rendered the collection of primary data in all countries in this study difficult. In several of the countries within this study, including Pakistan and Sri Lanka, few in-depth studies had been undertaken with regard to child sexual abuse and child sexual exploitation, adding to the difficulty in dealing with the subject matter openly. All reports in this study indicate the need for more comprehensiv, in-depth research.

Sexual abuse and sexual exploitation are coloured by deep-seated secrecy and denial, making it difficult to obtain primary or secondary data across the subregion. Many of the children interviewed were introverted and reluctant to talk about themselves and their health problems, especially with unfamiliar people. In the interviewing process, it was sometimes difficult to establish trust because of the limited time allotted for the study. This constraint made it difficult to observe children's behavioural trends over a sufficiently long period of time. Some of the information collected, therefore, is based largely on the respondent's mood and the situation at the time of the interview. The researchers, therefore, had to rely, to some extent, on service providers and care givers to provide information about the psychological and health problems of the children.

It is also noteworthy that all the primary data for the report on India was collected in Mumbai; only secondary data was used as a source for reporting on other parts of India.

For these reasons, and because of the limited number of children interviewed, this report can provide only an overview of the trends rather than conclusive data on the situation of child sexual abuse and sexual exploitation in the South Asian subregion.

Chapter II

Brief Situation Analysis of Child Sexual Abuse and Child Sexual Exploitation

Child sexual abuse and child sexual exploitation are some of the least acknowledged and least explored forms of child abuse in the South Asian subregion. It is clear from the national studies, however, that the problems of child sexual abuse and child sexual exploitation are widespread. In all the countries within the study the great majority of victims were nationals, although some were refugees or victims of extraterritorial trafficking (such as Nepalese children in India). The abusers were for the most part nationals of the country concerned, although in some countries, notably Sri Lanka, sex tourism was seen as a prevalent source of abusers.

Sexual exploitation of children very often had undertones of gender discrimination against females and this was even reflected in one country's laws. The exception was perhaps in Sri Lanka, where, at least in the commercial sexual exploitation of children, the vast majority of victims appeared to be boys. In all the countries within the subregion, however, both boys and girls were found to be victims of sexual abuse and exploitation.

All the countries within the subregion had legislation that criminalized both child sexual abuse and child sexual exploitation in some form, although these laws need to be strengthened or modified to bring them in line with international standards. The main problems with respect to laws revolved around the lack of enforcement which allowed the abuse of children to continue and perhaps even to increase.

The provision of health and social services to victims of sexual abuse and exploitation was very limited in all the countries in the subregion. Although the countries provided health services, sometimes to the hamlet level, these generally did not serve the victims' psychosocial needs. They tended to focus more on dealing with patients' immediate physical needs and on trying to prevent the spread of sexually transmitted diseases (STDs), including the human immuno-deficiency virus/acquired immune deficiency syndrome (HIV/AIDS). Other state institutions that catered to children seemed to focus on remanding them in custody on the orders of a court and sometimes providing them with formal and/or informal education. Few of these institutions, however, had the capacity, or the inclination, to address the psychosocial needs of these children or to help them recover from their trauma and reintegrate them into society.

In general, the health and social services available to child victims of sexual abuse and exploitation within the subregion are grossly inadequate. NGOs and private practitioners appeared to be the only providers of recovery and reintegration services to victims of child sexual abuse and exploitation. Even in these cases, and notwithstanding the commitment and efforts undertaken, the quality of the services provided varied greatly from one organization to another.

What follows is a brief overview of the situation in each country within the study, with a specific focus on the state of child sexual abuse and exploitation. For a more comprehensive review of each country, please refer to the full country report.

A. BANGLADESH

1. Child sexual abuse

There is a lack of awareness of the issue of child sexual abuse in Bangladesh and a lack of appropriate measures to combat and prevent ill-treatment and abuse, both within and outside the family. The matter is compounded by the lack of awareness of and information on abuse in such forms as domestic violence and early marriage. Some forms of sexual abuse of children include the early marriage of the girl child, abuse of children employed as domestic workers and in export-oriented factories, and abuse within a wide range of intra- and extra-familial relationships.

The prevalence of sexual abuse of children is a highly sensitive subject in Bangladesh, and pioneering work has been carried out by a group of volunteers called "Breaking the Silence". The data available, though limited, suggest that the incidence of sexual abuse of children cuts across class and affects all strata of society, but to no lesser or greater degree than in other societies.

Some of the findings made by "Breaking the Silence" were:

(a) With respect to sexual abuse it appears that no age is a safe age. Children are always vulnerable, but the highest number of abuses occur in children from 10 to 14 years of age. In the survey conducted for this study the mean age of the first incidence of sexual abuse was 11.57; children have been known, however, to be abused at as early an age as five;

(b) Girls are more vulnerable than boys. Furthermore, the abuse is compounded by being ostracized by society through its customs and censures. Especially in rural society, concern for the status quo often allows family pressures and social prestige to override the safety and well-being of abused children;

(c) Sexual abuse is more likely committed by the powerful than the powerless. It appears that the powerful may deliberately choose the powerless to abuse and children are often abused as a result of emotional dependence. Furthermore, children submit to the will of their families and in some cases willingly suffer abuse in order to preserve peace in the family. This behaviour is even more likely when such considerations are laced with economic dependency;

(d) Access to the victims is critical for committing abuse. Most abusers are those persons who have contact with the abused without arousing fear and suspicion. A rudimentary analysis shows that in 32 per cent of the cases, the abuse was committed by family members; in 46 per cent it was committed by people close to the family, such as home tutors and neighbours; and in 14 per cent of the cases it was by other known individuals. Abuse by total strangers accounted for only eight per cent of the cases.

Some other findings on child sexual abuse in Bangladesh include (the figures indicating the percentage among those interviewed):

(a) 13 per cent were abused by an employer's son;

(b) 78 per cent of male victims of sexual abuse were abused by strangers, while female victims were more often abused by their neighbours, gangs, or their husbands;

(c) The mean age of a child's first incidence of sexual abuse was 10.07 for males and 12.55 for females.

2. Child sexual exploitation

Most victims of child sexual exploitation in Bangladesh were brought to the city by someone from their village, most commonly a woman, with the promise of a job. After a few weeks of hardship in the streets these same women lured the children into the sex trade, as the easiest and fastest way of earning a living. Those who visited their homes usually told their families that they were employed as domestic workers.

Research indicates that of those engaged in the sex trade (the figures indicating the percentage of those interviewed):

(a) 68 per cent were unwillingly forced into it;

(b) 40 per cent of the male sex workers willingly joined the sex trade after they were persuaded into homosexual activity with friends;

(c) 47 per cent of the female sex workers were sold to pimps.

Whether they are brought into the sex trade willingly or unwillingly, a common perception is that once the children, both boys and girls, have been "spoiled", they are not accepted by society.

From a health perspective, 69 per cent of the victims suffered from STDs, 54 per cent suffered from syphilis and 17 per cent from skin diseases. Abdominal pain, vaginal discharge and infection of the sex organs were also common. Although most of them used some form of contraception, 67 per cent of the girls became pregnant, mostly by clients. Of those who became pregnant, 57 per cent gave birth.

The only semi-government survey of commercial sexual exploi-tation that was available was "Potita Jorip", or "Survey of Female Prostitutes", edited and published by the Department of Social Welfare. The scope of the survey was limited to the brothels of Dhaka and Narayanganj and did not take into account street sex workers. This survey found 1,259 prostitutes in the two cities.

Data maintained by the NGOs were more readily available for commercial than for non-commercial sexual abuse and exploitation. Data collected indicated that in 1997 some 820 children (both boys and girls) were trafficked. Additionally, in 1997 a total of 753 cases of rape had been recorded by ASK, and during the first quarter of 1998 some 202 rape cases resulting in nine deaths were reported. Other NGOs have been collecting data on commercial street sex workers in metropolitan areas.

The situation of sexually abused and exploited boys is mostly ignored by government agencies, except in the case of trafficking which receives a great deal of publicity due to the prevalence of trafficking in young boys to the Middle East for the purpose of camel jockeying.

Although the information available on the incidence of child sexual abuse and sexual exploitation in Bangladesh is limited, it is sufficient to indicate a worrying trend that deserves further indepth analysis. It is also clear that among NGOs and providers of services to the victims, there is a growing awareness of the need to address the issue of non-commercial sexual abuse and exploitation.

B. INDIA

1. Child sexual abuse

As in other countries, children in India who are victims of sexual abuse are more often than not raped or abused by family members, close friends or relatives. Servants, teachers and babysitters are also known to have abused children under their care.

Sexual abuse can harm the psychological health of the child. In addition to suffering from the trauma of abuse, sexually abused children are stigmatized by Indian society. They then grow up carrying the heavy burden of this label, which often contributes to their decision to enter prostitution. A related issue is that adolescent girls who are victims of sexual abuse often become pregnant as a result, contributing to a growing incidence of young, unwed mothers.

2. Child sexual exploitation

The estimated number of children in prostitution in India's metropolitan cities varies. Figures range from 270,000 to 400,000. The exact figure will no doubt never be known, but it is clear that there are many children being sexually exploited in India. By most estimates, about 20 per cent of these children are brought in annually from Nepal.

The factors and reasons that bring children into sex rackets vary by region. In Goa, a growing number of paedophiles sexually exploit young children, especially boys. Increasing numbers of minors, both boys and girls, are also finding their way to the red light areas of the state and into seaside bars. There they are used to attract tourists and increase business for the hotel industry. The main suppliers of young girls to the Goa market are the poverty-stricken districts of rural Karnataka.

In the states of Karnataka, Maharashtra and Andhra Pradesh, the *Devadasi* system is prevalent. This allows the dedication of pre-pubescent girls to a particular deity of a temple. The traditional meaning of this was that the girls were to undertake religious work in the temple and might have a lifelong sexual relationship with one of the priests. Currently, *Devadasis* are sometimes sent into prostitution at the instigation of the priests who try to attract additional income to the temple. (Singh 1990). The system has degenerated to the extent that often these girls are sent directly to brothels. The dedication ceremony, when the girl is "married" to the goddess, is performed prior to the emergence of secondary sexual characteristics, but she does not begin to work as a prostitute until puberty. These girls are also auctioned to the highest bidder who obtains the right to the virginity of the girl. Many of these *Devadasis* are moved into the Mumbai sex market where they become fully-fledged prostitutes. In Tamil Nadu in the south, many children also find themselves in the brothels of Chennai under the pretext of religion.

In Gujarat, where the level of awareness about the gravity and magnitude of the problem is extremely low, the migration of women and children due to the closure of textile mills in Ahmedabad has exacerbated the problem. This migration has resulted in the employment of many children as domestic labourers, where they are often abused. Migrant children staying in institutions for children are also subject to increased risk of sexual abuse by the caretakers themselves. In some villages, such as Wadia, a traditional profession is prostitution.

In these villages, unlike in other parts of India, the birth of a girl is much rejoiced over. As soon as the girl reaches puberty she is introduced into prostitution, with her father and brothers working as pimps for her.

In Madhya Pradesh, children of the Bancharas of Malwa and the Bedias of Bundelkhand, two communities with very low literacy rates, are pushed into prostitution with community approval. In Orissa, economic compulsions have led to the selling of children into prostitution. The states of Bihar and Uttar Pradesh in the north have the tradition of *tawaifs* (dancing girls) which in many cases has degenerated into the practice of prostitution.

According to a Workshop on Sexual Exploitation and Trafficking of Children held in 1996, in Punjab, Haryana, Chandigarh and Delhi, children from good socio-economic backgrounds have been reported to be involved in sex networks as a result of a desire for easy money. An accurate picture of the magnitude of the problem in Punjab, Haryana, Himachal Pradesh, Jammu and Kashmir, and Chandigarh cannot be given as no documented source is available.

Child trafficking for sexual exploitation

To meet the increasing demand for children in the sex trade, children are brought from the rural, poverty-stricken areas of India and also imported into India from Bangladesh, Nepal and other adjacent countries. Twenty per cent of all the women trafficked from Nepal were below 14 years of age. (CWIN 1998). In many areas of Bangladesh and Nepal, the level of poverty is so distressing that parents of young girls often either sell one of their daughters in order to secure two meals a day for the rest of the family or are duped into believing that their daughters will be married to well placed young men in India. Mumbai, Calcutta and Delhi are the most prominent destinations for traffickers, but other cities in India, particularly border towns, play an important role as well. (UNICEF 1997).

Trafficking of girls from India to the Gulf states and Europe is also common. Many middle-aged men come to India to "marry" minor girls of 13 to 18 years of age and then take them home to the Gulf states. Certificates for these marriages are easily obtained for a price. These girls are then coerced into being sex slaves or sold for a higher price.

Sex tourism and trafficking cannot be discussed separately as they are interlinked. Two studies conducted in the past have suggested that men are more likely to engage in sexual activities with children while they are away from home. Not only does the fact of being on holiday give greater licence, but the rules of the host society do not have so great a deterrent effect as those in which the man was socialized. Furthermore, the lack of rigid rules and the vulnerability of poor children in India give these men more leeway than they have at home.

C. NEPAL

1. Child sexual abuse

Child abuse has been a part of social reality in Nepal for generations. However, the sexual abuse of children remains largely hidden. Sometimes social values and cultural pressures discourage women and child victims from reporting abuses because they are afraid of humiliation, neglect and oppression by their family members and society.

In Nepal the number of reported cases of sexual abuse of children has shown an alarming increase recently, even though most of the cases go unreported. According to the survey conducted by Child Workers in Nepal (CWIN), young girls and women are regularly subjected to obscene remarks and other sexual harassment and abuse, including rape, by male co-workers and management staff. Such phenomena are particularly common in the carpet industry, where young girls are frequently victims of rape and sexual violence. (Pradhan 1993). Approximately 15 per cent of the rape incidents registered in the police department involve carpet factory workers.

According to the Crime Research Branch, 40 per cent of rape incidents go unreported, but lawyers and female social workers estimate that as many as 70 per cent go unreported. Incidents of abuse and rape are acknowledged only when the victims report them or others concerned know of the event. More than 50 per cent of all rape victims were girls under the age of 16, raped by their relatives. Marital rape is also common in Nepal, but is rarely reported.

Between November 1995 and December 1996, local newspapers reported a number of rape cases, 61 per cent of which occurred in girls under 16 and four per cent of which occurred in girls under 10. The perpetrators included neighbours, parents, relatives, teachers and employers. (Pradhan 1998). Many child domestic workers, especially girls, were also sexually exploited and abused. In some cases, the cycle perpetuates itself as these children go on to abuse the children of their employers.

A study conducted by Social Watch Group in 1996 reveals that children often enter the sex trade after they have been raped by street boys, squatters, porters or petty criminals. Of 50 children in the study, 12 reported that they were also sexually abused by police officers.

2. Child sexual exploitation

The sexual exploitation of children in Nepal is a very old phenomenon, older, in fact, than commercial sex work. Although prostitution and human trafficking are illegal, they occur in the country in a variety of forms. Sex work has been growing rapidly in the last few years. Most of the commercial sex workers enter and remain in the profession by compulsion or force of one form or another, not by their own free will. There are some girls and women, however, who have entered the profession through their own free choice.

The problem of child prostitution is spreading all over the country, predominantly in urban centres. These child sex workers operate in local hotels, lodges, rented rooms, their own rooms or huts, friends' rooms, their work place, and even near highways and inside vehicles. Customers are mainly local businessmen, soldiers, teachers, college students, politicians and even police officers. The commercial sexual exploitation of Nepalese children occurs in the following forms:

(a) Child trafficking

It is estimated that every year about 5,000 to 7,000 young girls from different parts of the country are trafficked into India, many of them lured through offers of employment opportunities in the garment and carpet industries. According to CWIN, about 200,000 Nepali prostitutes are in Indian cities, 20 per cent of whom are under the age of 16. (Pradhan 1998).

(b) Child prostitution

Some girls and women have adopted prostitution as their full-time occupation. For the most part, homeless girls and girls from poor or lower-middle class backgrounds fall into this category. A survey conducted by the Child Protection Centre – Nepal estimated that there are 800 such girls in the Kathmandu valley.

Other girls adopt prostitution as a secondary source of income. Girls and women who hold small jobs or have marginal incomes, those who come from the middle class, students and female labourers in carpet or garment factories have been found operating as prostitutes. About 300 such prostitutes are estimated to be involved in commercial sex work.

Prostitution is also adopted by members of the rich and privileged classes who take it on as a fashion or as entertainment, often under western cultural influences. The number of such sex workers is estimated to be around 1,000. (Child Protection Centre – Nepal 1994: 48).

(c) Cultural forms of sexual exploitation

The customs of the Badi, Deuki and Jhuma ethnic groups, still prevalent in various parts of the country, force girls into cultural forms of prostitution. Traditionally limited to the red light districts of western Nepal, where prostitution is socially accepted as a means of survival for the Badi and Deuki, the practice has now spread to other parts of the country as well. It is common in the Badi community for a man to involve his wife and daughters in commercial sex work in order to support the family. It is reported that 35 to 40 per cent of the Badi women involved in prostitution are girls under the age of 15.

(d) Sex tourism

Sex tourism is on the rise in Nepal, including an increasing incidence of paedophilia, as the business appears to be shifting to Nepal from other countries in South and South-East Asia. Paedophiles often attract street children by providing them with food, shelter, clothing and education. The children are then forced to maintain sexual relations with the providers. As they become used to the practice, however, some of the children continue in the sex trade for monetary gain.

(e) Sex slavery

Bonded families are bound to work for creditors from whom the family has borrowed money to deal with their economic problems, and these masters frequently sexually exploit the girls and women of the bonded family. Because of their indebtedness and helplessness the victims cannot protect themselves or revolt against their masters, nor can they reveal the exploitation they suffer.

Domestic workers are also used for sexual satisfaction by their employers as well as their employers' friends. However, the victims dare not report the incidents to the police or public agencies for fear of losing their livelihood.

D. PAKISTAN

1. Child sexual abuse

Though no statistical data are available, based on the interviews and data collected in the national study, one can reasonably conclude that child sexual abuse is prevalent in Pakistan. Child sexual abuse is probably the least acknowledged and least explored form of child abuse in Pakistan. This may be due to the taboo associated with the issue and to the fact that such matters continue to be viewed as domestic affairs. Only cases of particular cruelty and violence are reported by the media or acted upon by the police.

A study was undertaken in 1997 by the United Nations Children's Fund (UNICEF) in collaboration with the NGO Coalition on Child Rights on child sexual abuse in the North-West Frontier Province. It showed that the local newspapers, while not officially confirmed, reported 46 cases of child sexual abuse in that province during a three-month period. These cases included individual sexual assaults, gang rapes and incidents of incest and children being exposed to pornographic materials. The youngest victim was four years old.

It appears that many children are at risk of sexual abuse. Based on the interviews carried out in all the provinces, girls are most at risk of abuse by family members, acquaintances and neighbours, whereas boys seem to be more at risk of being molested by teachers and total strangers. The child victims are young. Though the statistical information is too small to draw definite conclusions, it is notable that in cases in which the age of the first incident of abuse was known, some 51 per cent of the victims interviewed in the study were 10 years old or younger, and 14.3 per cent were as young as five years old.

2. Child sexual exploitation

Owing to cultural and religious influences, the commercial sexual exploitation of children in Pakistan is kept underground. Its existence, however, is well known and acknowledged by many sectors of society, including law enforcement. As in other countries in the region, it is difficult to quantify the scope and scale of the problem. Boys are often more visible victims than girls, but this should not be taken as an indication that prostitution is more prevalent among males than females. It is more likely to be an indication of the level of public tolerance for male prostitution over female prostitution. Boys can be found at bus stands, hotels and restaurants, while girls tend to be prostituted from private homes and in the dancing business.

Little systematic research has been done to try to identify who the clients of either male or female prostitution are. Based on the information collected by the provincial studies undertaken under the ESCAP project, however, it appears that the most common clients include hotel owners, bus drivers, teachers, employers and police officers.

The commercial sexual exploitation of children in Pakistan can be divided into three categories as follows:

(a) Girls sold or married for profit

The legal age of majority for girls in Pakistan is 16, but marriages often take place at younger ages. In some parts of the country it is customary to obtain bride money at the time of marriage, though payment may not always be in cash.

(b) Female prostitutes

Prostitution is illegal in Pakistan, but as noted above, it is prevalent in the country and is most often conducted under the guise of dancing businesses. Traditionally, these businesses operate legally in the red light areas of the major cities, but commercial sex is an essential part of the lives of the girls they employ. Over the years many of the "traditional" dancing girls have been replaced by prostitutes engaged solely in selling their bodies.

Another form of prostitution is operated by elderly former prostitutes. These women rent houses in the cities to accommodate girls from the suburbs and adjoining towns, who stay for short periods of time for business. These "Naikas", as they are known, also encourage young women of the lower-middle class to join them. A third form of prostitution involves more exclusive upper class "call girls".

There is a premium placed on virginity, and in Pakistan it is typically sold at an early age. The price of a "Nath Utrai" or "first night" is much higher than the typical rate.

18

(c) Male prostitutes

The two most common categories of young male prostitutes are those working at small roadside hotels and bus stands, and the ones offering massage services. Most male prostitutes are reportedly first sexually abused between the ages of 12 and 15. Male prostitutes were found in all areas studied.

E. SRI LANKA

1. Child sexual abuse

Reports of sexual abuse of children in Sri Lanka have increased recently. It is not clear, however, whether this increase reflects a greater incidence of abuse or merely a higher rate of reporting as a result of the increased attention the issue has recently received. This phenomenon has not been adequately investigated because of the hidden nature of the problem.

The national study reveals that both boys and girls are subject to sexual abuse, although the abuse of girls appears more prevalent in Sri Lankan society. Some 92 per cent of the victims interviewed for the report were girls. Of these 92 cases (100 cases were interviewed), 61 were cases of rape while the rest involved other forms of sexual abuse.

Child victims of sexual abuse come from all ethnic groups and all religious faiths in Sri Lanka. The majority of victims ranged from 12 to 15 years of age, but as many as 10 per cent were between six and nine years old, while two per cent were children under the age of three.

In addition to being victims of incest, children were often sexually abused when they worked as domestic servants or were abandoned by parents who had gone abroad in search of employment. These children were left with relatives such as uncles and grandfathers who sometimes sexually abused them. In some cases, young girls who have been sexually abused by uncles or older cousins, or even by their own fathers, became pregnant and were forced to have abortions by folk medical means. In other cases they may secretly have borne children, who would be brought up within the family circle but without the acknowledgement of the father's identity.

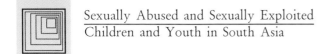

2. Child sexual exploitation

Child prostitution in Sri Lanka remains very much invisible. In the late 1970s, foreigners began to travel to Sri Lanka in increasing numbers, some of them seeking sexual relations with young boys, giving a new shape to the problem of child prostitution.

In the 1980s the Government of Sri Lanka appointed a Review Committee to create laws to prevent this new form of commercial sexual exploitation of children. Reports written by Tim Bond and several others commissioned by the government thereafter further revealed that children as young as ten, mostly boys, were being sexually exploited by paedophiles entering the country on tourist visas.

The demand for younger and younger victims is now evident. Old myths, such as the notion that sex with a pre-pubescent child can cure venereal diseases, and even HIV/AIDS, fuel the problem. The paedophiles who drive this demand believe that no STDs will be transmitted because young boys and girls are perceived to be "clean".

In Sri Lanka there are two types of child prostitution:

(a) Beach boys

Male prostitutes are usually self-employed and work either alone or in gangs, though it is possible to find male brothels run by small hotel or guesthouse operators. The self-employed boys practise their trade in the beach resort areas along the west and south-west coasts. Their ages generally range from eight to 15 years old. Young male prostitutes are usually dropouts from school working for a little money and have been lured into prostitution by the prospect of quickly and easily earning money.

Many of these "beach boys" come from fishing hamlets or coastal villages. While many are extremely poor, about 30 per cent of them are from stable middle-class backgrounds but have been lured into prostitution by agents who slip into their villages to recruit them. The agents promise the "dream" of "adoption" by a foreigner, who will take the child away to Europe, North America or Australia. That not one per cent receives such an opportunity is unknown to the future victims because the boys who have become prostitutes rarely return to their homes.

(b) Bonded children

A problem that is far more difficult to investigate is that of bonded children, who are as young as five years of age. They are used in prostitution and pornography and are controlled by strong international rings that cannot be easily penetrated. Most of the victims of this kind of exploitation come from poor homes in and around the tourist areas, although many are trafficked into these areas by agents and pimps. They are brought from rural villages with the prospect of employment but are lured into prostitution by unscrupulous agents.

The fate of the bonded child is bleak. Young victims are often discarded after a season or two, doomed to a life of crime thereafter. In addition, they are often injected with hormones and drugs, and become addicted to drugs or alcohol. Unless these victims are removed from their abusive environment at an early age, it is very difficult to ensure their effective rehabilitation.

The perpetrators of these crimes of sexual exploitation are usually foreign paedophiles, mostly German, Swiss, Dutch and French. In recent years, however, local "new rich" paedophiles have emerged, largely exploiting girls between the ages, of 12 and 16.

Chapter III

Children's Health Needs

A. HEALTH NEEDS OF SEXUALLY EXPLOITED AND SEXUALLY ABUSED CHILDREN

The public response in the South Asian subregion to child sexual abuse has often been fragmented and poorly coordinated. A significant public health problem stemming from child sexual abuse and exploitation demands a comprehensive social response. Before an appropriate response can be made, however, it is important to acknowledge and understand the problem, a task that both professionals and the community at large have been reluctant to undertake.

As noted earlier, it is important to recognize that victims and potential victims of sexual abuse and exploitation are in great need not only of health services but also of social services, including psychological and career counselling. Social development personnel play a critical role in preventing abuse and exploitation as well as in the victims' recovery and reintegration into society. They are in direct contact with the target group through the provision of services such as education and health care and are, therefore, in a position to address the specific needs of the target group.

This section provides an overview of the health needs that both sexually exploited and sexually abused children encounter resulting from their traumatic experiences, as documented by the various national studies.

The national reports describe a range of serious physical, social and psychological consequences for children of sexual abuse and sexual exploitation. Key elements of the reports' findings are summarized below.

1. Consequences of sexual abuse

The basic premise that children have a fundamental right to their personal integrity and to freedom from exploitation and abuse follows not only from international and national laws in the countries of South Asia, but also from the certainty that violation of these rights damages the children concerned. The most distressing consequences include physical and developmental problems and profound psychological and emotional disturbances.

2. Physical problems

Physical problems encountered by victims of child sexual abuse and exploitation can be categorized into two forms. The first form consists of those ailments directly linked to the abuse. The second consists of problems indirectly linked to the abuse or resulting from the victims' poor socio-economic situation.

(a) Direct results of sexual abuse and exploitation

Physical problems include bruises and bite marks on breasts and buttocks, unwanted pregnancies and lesions or infections in the vagina or anus. Victims also report frequent back problems. Illegal abortions are a common problem, particularly those performed by unqualified health practitioners resulting in vaginal bleeding and even infertility. Often, there is vaginal discharge indicating infection. Various skin infections, such as scabies, were also found among the victims.

(b) Problems indirectly linked to sexual abuse and exploitation

Most victims of sexual exploitation and abuse seemed to have frequent fits of coughing, colds, fevers and nasal tract infections. Some suffered from tuberculosis. Other complaints included intestinal problems, worms and lice. Frequent headaches were also common, though these may be attributable to other problems such as malnutrition and stress.

The above would seem to indicate a generally poor state of health of child victims of sexual exploitation and abuse. Some of their ailments may be because they come from poor backgrounds with poor hygienic conditions, but they are also signs of the stress and trauma caused by the sexual abuse. These children are in dire need of assistance to begin to address the physical traumas from which they suffer and to treat the psychological traumas discussed below.

3. Sexually transmitted diseases (STDs)

All national studies make reference to the presence of STDs among victims of sexual abuse and exploitation. The level of information, however, varies greatly from study to study. In Pakistan, for example, none of the children in the study were tested for STDs, even though almost none of the children ever used condoms to protect themselves. However, when the victims were asked whether they had experienced vaginal discharge, ulcers, pain during intercourse or pain in their lower back, almost one third of those interviewed in Karachi said they had experienced some of these symptoms.

The Indian study refers to the presence of STDs, including HIV/AIDS, but provides no statistical information. The Nepal study states that girls in a CWIN home all had at least one STD. Most of them had suffered from STDs such as syphilis, gonorrhoea, venereal warts, and infections of the urinary tract at least once in their lives. HIV infection and AIDS were also found among the victims of sexual exploitation in Nepal. Health-care workers have reported that around four per cent of the high-risk sex workers in Nepal suffer from HIV/AIDS.

According to an integrated community and industrial development initiative study conducted under the ESCAP project, a survey of commercially sexually exploited street children in Bangladesh found that 69 per cent had STDs, with 54 per cent suffering from syphilis and 17 per cent from skin diseases. There was also a prevalence of abdominal pain, vaginal discharge and infections of the sex organs. The Sri Lankan report refers to HIV/AIDS cases as well, though it does not provide any indication of the scope of this or other STDs.

The information in the national studies points to the need for greater awareness of the dangers of STDs, and HIV/AIDS in particular, including how people can best protect themselves. In addition, condoms should be freely distributed as widely as possible in order to remind people of their importance and encourage their use.

4. Psychological and emotional impact

Child sexual abuse and exploitation, whatever their forms, have a profound impact on the lives of victims – both as children and as adults later on. As the Bangladesh study points out, "any abused child is a traumatized child and that is an inescapable fact". The psychological consequences of sexual abuse of children can be even more dangerous than the physical effects. The children in the studies were often found to be suffering from psychological problems, reflected in falling grades, staring into space and difficulty in communicating. They also showed other behavioural problems such as temper tantrums, aggression, anxiety, guilty feelings and depression.

For the most part, the psychological and emotional effects of sexual abuse and sexual exploitation are similar, with the noted exception of children who are abused by a parent or close relative. In these cases there is the additional trauma of having been abused by someone the child trusted. Pained by the sense of betrayal, these children often have difficulty building trusting relationships later in their lives.

Child sexual abuse and exploitation involve violations of the victim's body, privacy, honour and rights to independence and autonomy. Such violations have immediate and long-lasting effects. The issues of repressed anger and hostility and the failure to accomplish normal developmental tasks are all particularly significant. Unless the victims receive appropriate help and support, their prospects for avoiding the destructive consequences of abuse and exploitation are poor.

The treatment and reintegration of victims is a highly technical and demanding task. Many experts believe that the profound psychological impact of sexual abuse on the children may render them more likely to abuse other children in the future. Treatment is also, therefore, a means of prevention, reducing the risk of victims becoming perpetrators.

In order for victims to recover and be reintegrated into their families and society, they need professional counselling. Such counselling may need to be supported by medical treatment to bring the children back to health. There is also a strong need for respect and acceptance (as opposed to stigmatization) within their communities. In the case of victims of sexual abuse, there is also the need to be believed. All victims need to be provided with viable alternative job opportunities through education and vocational training. Finally, all the victims need unconditional love and acceptance, particularly as they are often judged to be responsible for their own abuse and as a result feel dirty, low and rejected.

B. HEALTH AND SOCIAL SERVICES

The level of services available in the subregion varies greatly from country to country. Most national health services are aimed at addressing the physical problems of the victims and at preventing the spread of infections and STDs. In all the countries in the study there is recognition of the need to develop a greater capacity to deal with the recovery and reintegration of victims of sexual abuse and exploitation and to build on existing services. These good intentions, however, are hampered by limited resources. Perhaps the most important development in this area is the recognition of the problem and the needs that flow from it.

The services provided by NGOs and other members of the public also vary greatly from country to country. There appears to be a stronger presence of NGOs dealing with the recovery and reintegration of victims in Bangladesh, India and Nepal, whereas organizations addressing these issues appear to be fewer in Pakistan and Sri Lanka. In Nepal for example, the majority of NGOs and reintegration centres observed had their own health clinics and most of the centres had both counselling and treatment facilities for sexually exploited and abused children. In Sri Lanka only seven organizations nationwide were identified in the report that provided such care services.

1. Physical problems

In all the countries in the study, the national health services, NGOs and private practitioners cater to the physical needs of children who have been sexually abused or exploited. The main issues revolving around these services are their quality and scope, and the need for the provision of services at low cost since the victims are rarely in a position to seek expensive treatment. Many victims of sexual abuse and exploitation seek the help of unqualified practitioners because of the prohibitive cost of professional services.

Another issue is the tendency for victims not to seek medical assistance until the symptoms of their problem are acute. This is linked to the fear that their abuse or exploitation will become known as well as their fear of the law due to the illegal nature of sex work. There is a need to find the means to enable the victims to feel more comfortable in seeking medical assistance and to ensure them of the confidentiality of such treatment.

2. Psychological and emotional impact

Perhaps the area needing the greatest development is the provision of services addressing the psychological and emotional needs of child victims of sexual abuse and exploitation. Though some excellent services are available in all countries in the subregion, it may be concluded from the study that the availability, cost and quality of these services could be significantly improved.

In Sri Lanka, for example, few NGOs provide institutional or residential rehabilitative care for victims of sexual exploitation. Those that do provide such services generally do not have sufficiently qualified counsellors or adequate infrastructure. These institutions are also unable, due to limited finances and expertise, to provide the vocational training necessary to provide alternatives to the sex trade. It is important that the Sri Lankan Government focus on this aspect of reintegration, as the Department of Probation and Childcare Services has generally tended to concentrate more on "probation", than on "childcare services".

In Nepal, on the other hand, the majority of NGOs and reintegration centres observed had their own health clinics in which health assistants and nurses provided general services to the children. Most NGOs and reintegration centres provided food, clothing and shelter to the children who stayed there. They also provided recreation, such as indoor games, music and dancing. Some of the children who had music and dance training in the centres were able to find employment in hotels and restaurants and could earn money to support themselves and their families.

Some of the children received psychological treatment aimed at reintegrating them into their families and society, as well as giving them confidence about their social and economic needs. That being said, institutions providing such services are still too few and too ill equipped to meet the needs of a growing number of victims.

In India, services are available to meet some of the needs of the victims, but there are gaps in these services. They are generally of a curative nature and may succeed in meeting the victims' medical needs. They provide counselling, education and vocational guidance. In some of the organizations doing commendable work, however, the quality of the services depends largely on the skills of individual workers. The services provided would suffer if these key workers left the organization.

In Pakistan, there are few organizations providing recovery and reintegration services to victims of sexual abuse and exploitation, though various human rights groups and NGOs provide shelter and legal advice. There is a great need to build the capacity to provide health and psychosocial services that address the growing needs of the victims, at least in the major cities.

The Bangladesh report highlights the lack of awareness of sexual abuse, particularly among public service providers. It goes on to express the need for training and building human resources to help address the issues of sexual abuse and exploitation. It also notes the marked differences in attitudes between the public service providers and NGOs, with the latter appearing to have a greater awareness of the issues and a greater commitment to addressing them.

There is a clear need across the subregion to strengthen the services provided to child victims of sexual abuse and exploitation. The capacity of public agencies and NGOs must be improved so that they will be able to provide children with food, shelter, education and health care. Counselling and assistance with reintegration into their families and society should also be emphasized and supported. Finally, service providers should be able to offer career counselling and vocational training so that sexually abused and exploited children will be able to earn a livelihood outside the sex trade.

Chapter IV

Conclusions and Recommendations

A. CONCLUSIONS

1. General conclusions

1. From the findings in the national reports it can be said with certainty that the problem of child sexual abuse and commercial sexual exploitation of children exists and is prevalent in all five countries of the South Asian subregion covered under this report.

2. The problem of child sexual abuse and sexual exploitation remains hidden in most of the countries in the South Asian subregion because of social norms and values. In Pakistan and Sri Lanka, for example, there are no identifiable "red light" districts such as the ones in some cities of South-East Asia.

3. Various studies identified many causes of sexual exploitation and abuse, but the most commonly identified ones included poverty, lack of education, lack of employment opportunities, the migration of women abroad to seek employment, broken families, and male-dominated social systems.

4. Building on this last point, it appears that social values that place women in a subordinate position to men contribute to the sexual abuse and exploitation of girls. It was noted that in some countries, the law did not provide the same rights to women and girls that it did to men.

2. Child sexual abuse and sexual exploitation

1. In all the countries in the study it appeared that children were sexually abused mostly at the hands of known or trusted people, including relatives and teachers.

2. Victims of sexual abuse commonly included street children, child domestic workers, child labourers in sweat shops such as carpet factories, hotels or small restaurants, assistants to bus or truck drivers, and children in other similar occupations.

3. Based on these studies, the majority of victims of sexual abuse and exploitation, both girls and boys, were in the range of 12 to 15 years old, though many of the victims were found to be much younger.

4. Although both girls and boys can be found in commercial sexual exploitation across the subregion, there appears to be greater visibility of one sex over the other in some countries. In both Pakistan and Sri Lanka boys seemed to be more visible in sexual abuse and exploitation than girls, while in Bangladesh, India and Nepal girls were more visible, especially in urban centres.

3. Health problems of sexually abused and sexually exploited children

1. The victims of sexual abuse and exploitation were seen to have physical injuries such as bruises, bite marks on breasts and buttocks, unwanted pregnancies and infections in the vagina or anus.

2. Illegal abortions were a common occurrence, particularly abortions performed by unqualified health practitioners resulting in post-surgery complications such as vaginal bleeding and damage to the reproductive organs. The consequences of such abortions also included vaginal discharge, indicating infection, and various skin infections, such as scabies.

3. Most victims of sexual exploitation and abuse seemed to have frequent fits of coughing, colds, fevers and nasal tract infections. Some were afflicted with tuberculosis, while others complained of intestinal problems, worms and lice.

4. Many of the victims were found to be suffering from STDs such as syphilis, gonorrhoea and HIV/AIDS infection. Some girls also suffered from uterine prolapses, puss and white discharge, while some boys had infected anal passages and urinary tracts.

5. The psychological and emotional effects of sexual abuse and exploitation were found to include depression, fear, mental disturbances, sleeping problems and low self-esteem. These and other psychological problems sometimes resulted in suicide and even murder.

4. Health service providers

The national studies highlighted the insufficiencies of the existing services provided to victims of sexual abuse and exploitation. The Sri Lankan report stated that few after-care services for victims of commercial sexual exploitation existed in the government sector. The Nepalese report noted that there were very few institutions, including NGOs, that provided services. Furthermore, the services available were inadequate, in terms of both quality and scope. In India, the research concluded that services were there to meet some of the needs of the victims but that gaps in the services were also present. The Pakistan report highlighted the availability of medical provisions of a curative nature but also recognized the lack of services aimed at helping victims recover and reintegrate into society. The Bangladesh report highlighted the strong need to develop the capacity of the public sector to deliver health services.

B. RECOMMENDATIONS

Though the focus of this report is on the health needs of child victims of sexual abuse and sexual exploitation, it is clear that the solutions to these complex problems are multi-disciplinary. The recommendations below, therefore, cover a variety of areas. They are seen to be relevant to all the countries within the sub-region. For more country-specific recommendations, please refer to the individual national reports. The recommendations have been organized into five groups: general recommendations; recovery and reintegration; prevention; protection; and cooperation and coordination.

1. General recommendations

1. Existing national policies and programmes should be thoroughly reviewed, leading to the formulation and implementation of comprehensive plans that meet the needs of child victims of sexual abuse and sexual exploitation and their families. These plans and the resultant policies need to be based on children's rights and respect for social justice.

2. The national governments and political parties within the subregion need to make an explicit commitment to these comprehensive plans for victims of child sexual abuse and sexual exploitation in order to ensure their success.

3. More resources should be allocated to the prevention of further child sexual abuse and sexual exploitation as well as to the recovery and reintegration of victims into society.

2. Recovery and reintegration

1. Reintegration strategies for victims of child sexual abuse and sexual exploitation should be developed that involve the national network of hospitals and health-care centres at the provincial, district and community levels in addition to national and international NGOs. These strategies should be implemented through a range of approaches, such as residential care, psychotherapy and community-based programmes that nurture and promote local support groups and networks. They should always seek to involve the immediate families of the victims as appropriate.

2. All services for the victims of sexual exploitation and sexual abuse must demonstrate respect for the child and be open and non-judgmental. These programmes can be effective and efficient only if they adopt participatory strategies involving the child, the family and the community.

3. If not already in place, programmes of recovery, psychosocial rehabilitation and reintegration of victims of child sexual abuse and exploitation should be established, at least in all major urban centres.

4. Facilities for formal and effective counselling for victims of child sexual abuse and sexual exploitation should be set up, keeping in mind the children's need for confidentiality.

5. Training programmes targeting medical staff, law enforcement officials, lawyers, judges and others involved in providing services to victims of sexual abuse or exploitation should be provided. Such training should be aimed at raising awareness of the issues and at making the participants aware of how to deal with the children as victims rather than as offenders and how to avoid inflicting further trauma on them.

6. Community support networks for victims of child sexual abuse and sexual exploitation should be established where they do not already exist and strengthened where they do.

3. Prevention

1. Each country in the South Asian subregion should consider awareness campaigns, developed and launched by the government in close collaboration with NGOs, using the media to highlight child sexual abuse and exploitation. Such campaigns should advocate against the trafficking of children for sexual purposes, sexual exploitation, sexual abuse and violence as well as informing the public of where help can be sought for both the children and the abusers. They should also be aimed at breaking down the taboos surrounding these issues and the stigmas attached to victims in order to facilitate their reintegration into society. Furthermore, they should aim at raising awareness of HIV and the spread of AIDS, and should reach the hamlet level, wherever possible.

2. Compulsory education for all children should be enforced throughout the South Asian subregion. The curriculum should cover children's basic rights as well as reproductive health in order to develop healthy attitudes towards sex, sex-related issues (such as safe sex) and STDs. The educational system should also be used to teach children how to avoid abuse and exploitation, and should target parents, teachers and social workers in addition to the children.

3. Teachers should be made especially sensitive to the issues of child sexual abuse and sexual exploitation so that they can help in detecting its occurrence.

4. National tourist boards should review and realign their marketing efforts to encourage responsible tourism and to discourage child sexual exploitation.

5.   Income generation schemes targeted at high-risk groups should be encouraged in order to reduce their poverty level and alleviate the need to resort to commercial sexual exploitation as a means of survival. Skills training should form an integral part of the income-generating process.

6.   More research should be undertaken in order to better understand the sexual abuse and exploitation of children and to improve the services to deal with them. Such research should focus on:

- Further effective, culturally sensitive measures that could be undertaken to prevent the sexual abuse and exploitation of children

- The exploitation of and violence against child domestic workers

- The sexual exploitation of adopted children

- Teachers' behaviour with children and youth with special reference to sexual abuse

- The need to motivate child prostitutes away from sex work

- The effectiveness of counselling techniques in rehabilitating sexually abused children

- The relationship between education and sex work, exploitation and abuse

4. Protection

1.   Though laws dealing with sexual abuse and sexual exploitation exist in all countries within the subregion, most of them need to be strengthened in various ways, including the following.

(a) Laws should cater specifically to child abuse and exploitation if they do not already do so explicitly;

(b) Laws should be more child-centred, treating them as victims rather than as offenders, taking the children's statements of abuse at face value and implementing child-friendly court procedures such as video link evidence presentation;

(c) In cases of sexual exploitation of children, the age defining a "child" should be in line with the Convention on the Rights of the Child (up to 18 years of age), as a child in an exploitative situation is not in a position to offer consent;

(d) Laws should grant abortion rights to young women who have conceived as a result of sexual abuse or exploitation;

(e) Laws on pornography should address new technological developments, should be defined in such a way as to include electronic pornography, and should criminalize its production, distribution and possession;

(f) Laws should be in line with the Convention on the Right of the Child, particularly Article 2, ensuring the equal treatment of girls and boys before the law, "irrespective of the child's or his or her parent's or legal guardian's race, colour, sex, language, religion, political or other opinion, national, ethnic or social origin, property, disability, birth or other status".

2. Existing laws pertaining to child sexual abuse and sexual exploitation should be strictly enforced by law enforcement agencies.

3. Extraterritorial legislation should be enacted that would allow for the prosecution of foreign nationals who violate the rights of local children.

4. Law enforcement personnel should be provided with training to increase their awareness of the causes of child sexual abuse and child sexual exploitation, as well as existing legislation and how best to implement it. The fact that abused or exploited children are victims and not offenders should be emphasized. Training should be carried out involving law enforcement agencies, NGOs and organizations involved in recovery and reintegration work as well as the legal and medical professions. This would contribute to a better understanding of the role of each party in the recovery of children from sexual abuse and exploitation and their reintegration into society.

5. Rescue operations aimed at removing children from prostitution should be coordinated with all relevant agencies in order to ensure that rescued children can be taken care of appropriately.

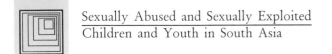

5. Cooperation and coordination

1. Child sexual abuse and exploitation are complex problems that demand a multidisciplinary and well integrated response. The development and implementation of strategies to deal with these issues should involve relevant members of the public sector, the private sector and civil society.

2. Networking and coordination among service providers, the government and law enforcement agencies should be made part of their routine operations, and should also form an integral part of any action plan to address child sexual abuse and sexual exploitation.

3. Organizations should be more open to sharing information with professionals working on child sexual abuse and sexual exploitation so that they can work together toward a comprehensive solution to the issue.

4. Programmes to combat child sexual abuse and sexual exploitation should be regularly monitored and evaluated to determine their effectiveness. The results of this evaluation should be shared with all those concerned on a regular basis so that programmes can be modified accordingly.

5. Income-generation schemes should be coordinated with government poverty alleviation programmes as well as microcredit schemes provided to the victims and potential victims' families at the grass-roots level.

Annexes

I. Case studies of individual victims

The case studies below have been selected from the many cases presented in the national reports. They are meant to provide samples of the kinds of sexual abuse and exploitation to which children are subjected. The names of the children and in some cases their precise locations have been altered to protect the victims.

Case study 1: Lalita Thapa

Lalita Thapa, a poor inhabitant of Syangja, is a good example how girls are sexually abused and compelled to enter into prostitution. Lalita is 16 years old and her family consists of a stepbrother, a step-sister-in-law and an elder sister. From her early childhood she was deprived of adequate food, shelter and education, as her family suffered extreme economic hardship, a situation that would have been different if her parents had been with her during her childhood. It is not surprising that Lalita, to whom the fundamental right to education has been totally denied, is illiterate.

Before entering commercial sex, Lalita worked as a labourer. Her earnings, however, could not support nor fulfil her basic needs. An incident from her youth illustrates how girls are used as sex objects, even by their own relatives and friends. One day Lalita was in the jungle cutting and collecting feed for the cattle. Her uncle came to her and threatened her, putting his hand over her mouth to make her silent. Since the place was very isolated in a jungle, she was compelled to surrender. Her own uncle raped her for the first time.

The second time she was abused, she was psychologically traumatized by her best friend, who had asked her to go with her to see a theatre programme. Instead of going to the theatre, she was carried to a room in a building in a very strange setting. There was a boy sitting inside the room. When Lalita entered the room the boy locked the door and raped her. After she had been raped twice, her friend told her that she could earn money selling her body for sexual purposes. Her destitute economic condition along with the tyranny at home compelled her to sell her body. She has now been working as a prostitute for one year.

As a commercial sex worker, Lalita has difficulty with group sex. Though sex is arranged with a single person, sometimes five to seven people come together and try to have sex with her simultaneously. In the end, they are sometimes even reluctant to pay the charges to which they have agreed. She also faces violent clients, some of whom like to use knives and force her to have sex.

Lalita knows very well of the social stigma of prostitution. She would like to quit the profession, but she sees no options. She is ready to start her own business if money can be made available, and she has been found to have a strong desire for permanent conjugal life if she can find somebody who can accept her.

Case study 2: Chandrika Dasanayake

The following first-hand account details an incident that occurred in 1996 in the Kurunegala district:

My name is Chandrika Dasanayake. I live at Elle Gedera. I attended Mahanama Vidyalaya. I am now 13 years of age. My father works for the Irrigation Department. The incident happened when my mother was in Kuwait. I have a brother older than me. When the incident happened I was 11 years old. I was in grade six. After the incident I did not go to school. The incident was known all over my village and I felt ashamed. When the incident happened my brother was 13 years of age. Now I am not concerned about the incident. Now I have forgotten about it. But how can I go to school again? The person who did this to me is Dharmadasa Seeya (Grandpa Dharmadasa). ["Seeya" is sometimes used to refer to the elderly.] The incident happened on 16 May 1996 at about three or four in the afternoon. There is a cashew nut tree near my home. It is somewhat like a jungle area. It happened under that tree when my mother was abroad and my father was at work. The only persons there were my brother and I. We would come back from school and stay at home till father comes home from work. My brother would go out to play cricket with his friends. Then only I was at home. Sometimes Dharmadasa Seeya would come to visit us. When he comes, we would start a conversation. I liked to sit on his lap. He lived just a couple of houses away from ours. Sometimes he would bring toffees, apples etc. He was very fond of me. On that day he came near the well and went to the boutique to buy some goods and wanted me to be near the cashew nut tree. There was no one at home at that time. I went near the cashew tree. Then he came there. He asked me to sit down. I sat down. Then he said, "Let us do." I said "no" and tried to go away. He held me and kept me on his lap. He asked me to remove my knickers. I removed them. He removed his sarong. I then saw his organ. He kept it near my organ and pressed it. It was painful and some blood came out. I was frightened. Then he kept his organ between my thighs and shook. He asked me not to tell anyone. When he saw there was blood he told me to go home and apply coconut oil. I did not do so. I was frightened and told my maternal aunt. She told my father when he returned. Then father went to the police station. A case was filed.

Researchers have analysed the factors leading to Chandrika's situation. Her mother had gone abroad about one year before this incident. There was evidence from outside the family that the relationship between the father and mother was weak, and the father was found to have had many extramarital affairs, even before the mother went abroad. When the researchers went to the house the mother was still in a foreign country and it was evident to them that in such a family environment, a child could easily be sexual prey.

In this case, it is necessary to pay special attention to the abuser, who is 65 years of age. His wife died nine years before the incident happened and he did not re-marry. He is the father of seven children. When he visits Chandrika's home he keeps the girl on his lap and caresses her, and he has sometimes had sex with her using her thighs. On the day she describes, he raped her. It was learned that he was punished in the courts and served a term in prison. He has been released, but has not come back to the area.

Case study 3: Tiramunige Palitha Samn Silva

This report is based on an unstructured interview with a boy by the name of Palitha Silva.

If my memory is correct my first sexual experience was with a man known as Kudu Seeya (hunchback grandpa), who begs close to the railway station. The incident is as follows. That day I slept outside the railway station near the canteen. It was raining heavily. About 11 at night this old man came near where I was sleeping and spread a cardboard sheet and slept. When I got up at about three or four in the morning he had removed my pants halfway. He got on top of me and moved fast up and down. He embraced me and said not to tell anyone of this incident. He gave me five rupees. Thereafter on a number of occasions I have received money from him like this. I have gone with older boys to the Beira Lake and I have had similar experiences. They go to the Beira Lake in the evenings between six and eight to catch fish.

The first time I had sex with a foreigner was at the Rest House in Fort. I went there with Samantha Aiyya ["Aiyya" is a term used for older boys]. One day he told me he would get me a lot of money and told me to come with him. I went with him to the hotel of the gentleman.   Then a white man known to Samantha Aiyya came to him and put his hand around his neck and spoke to him. He took us to the room. He kept me and asked Samantha to go. Samantha said you can have sex with this white man and earn a lot of money. At first I said no. Later all three of us remained in the room and had beer. We were thoroughly intoxicated. There were short-eats and we smoked cigarettes. Then Samantha Aiyya removed his pants and went near the white man. Then the white man touched Samantha and me. We also did the same for him and also massaged him. The white man, then, had sex with Samantha and me. We were given food to eat and Rs 500. He asked us to come again. I have had sex with the white man on seven or eight occasions. When sailors come we go to them and have sex and earn money. There are about five boys with me who go like this. One day I met a white man at Galle Face Green. He gave me Rs 100 and told me if I go with him to the hotel he will give me Rs 1,000. I went with him. At the security checkpoint our three-wheeler was stopped by the army. It was about 7 p.m. The Army people inquired where I was going and they chased me. He ran. I saw the three-wheeler moving. I have had sex with about 30 white men. I have not had sex with white women.

I have been in two children's homes. We have no freedom there. When we are on the road no one looks after us. My mother is addicted to drugs and she does not supervise me. Sometimes she takes the money I have. I also get money from her. A few of my friends were caught by the police stealing and they are at Kottawa Detention Home. When we need money we work in boutiques and earn money. There is no one to see how we are faring.

As far as illness is concerned, my genital area got infected. My mouth also got infected. I have received treatment from the hospital. I have a rash on my body and I have gone to private medical practitioners.

My future hope is to become a three-wheeler driver. Then I will buy a three-wheeler and behave well. Please do not give this information to the police or to the newspapers. The police will arrest us and send us to Kottawa Detention Home; we will suffer there.

II. CASE STUDIES OF SERVICE PROVIDERS

The case studies of service providers below are all taken from the India report. They were selected as examples because of the consistency with which these institutions were analysed. It was felt that they were representative of the type of institutions found in all the countries in the subregion and as such would serve well as illustrations. The names of the organizations have been withheld to assure their anonymity.

Organization A

(a) Structure of the organization

Founded in 1922, Organization A, known as a fit-person institution, has a residential approach to dealing with children and their problems. It is run by a religious order as a registered trust under the Bombay Trust Act and is managed by a president and a board of trustees of the order. The institution has cottages overseen by sisters of the congregation who work in coordination with the president. The cottages are residential quarters for the beneficiaries, mainly minor girls. The organization also runs a regular school for children from lower socio-economic backgrounds in the area as well as the children who live in the institution. The school has its own hierarchy consisting of a principal, vice-principal, teachers, administrative and service staff, and its work structure is different from that of the institution. On a parallel level, the institution has visiting doctors, a psychologist, a gynaecologist, a paediatrician, in-house nurses and a trained social worker from the congregation. The institution also has an infirmary, a cottage to house children with HIV/AIDS, a nursery for babies, and a chapel. Government grants, individual donors, philanthropists, and funds raised by the religious congregation are the institution's sources of funding. Educational grants from the Department of Education take care of the school budget of 3,300,000 rupees a year. The annual budget for the institution funded by the government is 950,000 rupees.

(b) Profile of children cared for

The organization offers its services to a wide range of children. They include destitute, abandoned and abused children; minor girls committed to the institution by the courts for rescue and prevention purposes; unmarried mothers (some are over 18 years of age) who come for delivery and post-delivery care and reintegration; and children suffering from HIV/AIDS. The children are often placed in the institution by the courts which instruct it under the Juvenile Justice Act to provide care and protection. Unmarried mothers do not need court directives for their stay, nor do the HIV/AIDS infected children. When the organization finds orphaned children who have no guardian, the workers take the children in and then approach the Juvenile Welfare Board to legalize their residence. The organization mainly serves girls, but male children are also sometimes cared for, for up to ten years. There are a total of 380 children in the residential cottages. They stay until reintegration is complete, which can take until the age of 25, by which time the girls either secure a job or get married and settle down.

(c) Personnel

Employees are appointed primarily on the basis of their motivation and commitment to the cause of children's development and well-being. Qualifications relevant to the specific requirements of each job are also important. Patience and understanding of the background and mental state of the children and youth being served are sought in potential personnel.

There are 52 school staff members and 57 in the institution itself, including the service staff. These include five social workers, four visiting doctors and four nurses. Preference is given to female or male staff depending on the job being filled. The staff from the religious order are not on the payroll but the rest of the staff are paid between Rs 3,000 and 8,000 a month depending on their number of years in service and training, while the visiting doctors receive a monthly honorarium of Rs 3,000. The teachers receive training and orientation in new developments in education. Sensitivity and childcare training workshops are held regularly for the staff and information is given on government and NGO childcare programmes. Literacy training is also provided for staff members who need it. A provident fund, rent for housing and loan facilities are some of the standard benefits offered to the staff, but their main motivation is the feeling of service towards a good cause.

(d) Services provided

The focus of the organization is on providing education, the aim being to make the girls independently employable. For this purpose formal education up to the tenth grade is provided in the school run by the organization. Those who join the institution at a later stage can obtain non-formal education. Opportunities for higher education, specialized training in a particular trade or skill, and job placement services are provided for the girls. The sheltered cottages of the institution provide them with health care and protection from an abusive environment. Health care is also extended to destitute or neglected babies. Unmarried women get pre- and post-natal care by trained nurses as well as access to hospitals and medical specialists. Adoption services as well as special care for HIV-positive children are also provided. The agency has recently ventured into providing care to sexually exploited and abused girls, especially those rescued from brothels.

(e) Achievements, constraints and future plans

The organization rates its achievements in terms of girls leaving the institution with a sense of independence and pursuing careers of their choice or getting married. Reunions organized by the institution for girls who have left are a source of pride for the organization, as the girls not only get to socialize with their old friends, but also receive more knowledge and skills through talks by professionals on child rearing, interpersonal relationships and new healing techniques such as naturopathy. The organization maintains good relationships with government bodies and neighbouring communities, which it views as important resources.

One major accomplishment of the organization was the reintegration of 160 prostitutes placed with them for six months by the state government in 1996. This gave them hands-on experience in handling such unexpected demands and in enhancing the former prostitutes' self image. This experience also made them determined to include services for minor prostitutes in their agenda. They are planning to open a halfway house to accommodate such children and to create more opportunities for them, giving them more options than returning home.

Due to time constraints and the constant need to attend to administrative and record keeping work, the agency finds it difficult to impart valuable education to the children. In addition, the agency staff needs training in how to impart such education in a way to which the children will be receptive.

46

Organization B

(a) Structure of the organization

This non-residential NGO was established in 1987 and consists of a shelter, a day-care centre and ten local contacts for outreach. It is run by a priestly order and consists of a director, two assistant directors, two social workers, two office staff and one handyman. No rigid hierarchy is followed although the director and the assistant directors are in charge. The para-professionals are chosen from among the beneficiaries themselves. The director oversees the overall functioning of the shelter. The two assistant directors are responsible for the financial and development work in the shelter and oversee the day-care centre and health issues, respectively. Funding depends mostly on individuals and donor organizations but they do not advertise for funds. They do not believe in large scale budgeting and funding, nor in seeking government or foreign funds. They avoid planning big programmes and think that funds will come when there is a felt need. No compromise is ever made on health-related tasks.

(b) Profile of children cared for

This organization is intended for street children and is only for boys, generally between the ages of five and 22. They come to the shelter on their own, especially when their friends recommend it as an open place without restrictions. Many children decide to stay at the shelter after attending its monthly *mela* (fair). Many of the children who grow up under the care of the shelter join in its work as para-professionals to help other street children. In order to minimize the exploitation of the younger boys by the older ones, the shelter's policy since 1995 has been that the upper age limit for staying is 14. Those already living at the shelter, however, are not asked to leave until they decide to. Now, there are more younger boys in the shelter than older ones. There are a total of approximately 100 to 130 boys at the shelter but this number increases during the monsoon season.

(c) Personnel

The essential criteria for selecting personnel are their commitment and an attitude of non-judgmental acceptance. Although for social worker positions, people with Masters in Social Work degrees are preferred, the management is looking into experimenting with training less qualified personnel to suit the job requirements. At present three members of a religious order form the management, and two social workers, two office staff and a handyman are employed by the organization. The rest of the staff are para-professionals who receive 1,500 rupees a month. They are selected from among those beneficiaries who have decided to contribute to the cause. For social workers, preference is given to women, in order to supplement the male staff who make up the management. These persons have to be young enough to face the challenges of the job and be willing to adapt to and understand the child's perspective.

The pay scale here is on a par with other NGOs. So far there are no staff benefits such as a provident fund or gratuities, but the management team has recruited volunteers to find out the benefits other NGOs are offering their staff so that they may offer standard compensation packages. The training of personnel is done informally on a one-to-one level. The social workers are given ample opportunities to coordinate with other NGOs and government bodies and to represent the organization at outside training programmes.

(d) Services provided

Three major services are provided by this agency. The first is a shelter for boys, for short-term as well as long-term stays. "Short-term" in this case is understood to mean that a child comes to the shelter for a couple of days, then leaves and probably returns another day. "Long-term" indicates that the child begins to recognize the shelter as his address and feels a sense of belonging. The second service, a day-care centre, is available for street children, including those with families living on the streets. It offers a canteen managed by the children, recreational activities, bath facilities and haircuts. The third service is an outreach, in which the staff, equipped with medical kits, scan the streets to identify children in need. With the timely intervention of this service, the organization has been able to help many children.

Under these broad services come other services of no less importance. The shelter provides the children with a scrap shop so that they can acquire certain skills to maintain their livelihood rather than fall into vices such as prostitution or drugs. A locker facility is another innovative service, giving the street children a place to keep precious possessions as well as a private space accessible only to them. Savings are also encouraged and children are introduced to banking facilities. The focus of all these services is on providing emotional security. The shelter also gives 50 children access to formal education, while providing others with non-formal classes and vocational training in more than a dozen skills or trades, including electrical work, plumbing and mechanical work. Job placements are also offered to the older boys.

(e) Achievements, constraints and future plans

The agency considers its scrap shop and locker facility major achievements in terms of having the desired effect. The monthly fair has proved to be a success even with children outside the shelter. The organization considers its open environment as its strength, giving children freedom, space, security and love. This same environment curbs the cultivation of vices. A research and documentation centre is being set up to access information and prepare documentation on street children and youth. They are also planning to expand their services to other areas of the city and even to other cities by way of a chain of shelters and day-care centres using the same child-centred approaches. The focus of the research centre will be to enable these ambitions to be fulfilled.

Organization C

(a) Structure of the organization

This special institution, a home for girls, was built by the government in 1958. Housed in the premises of this institution are two reception centres that cater to different target groups of children less than 18 years of age. It comes under the Department of Women and Child Development (WCD) of the state government. The hierarchy is distinct and consists of the director of the WCD department, deputy director, divisional officer, district officer, superintendent, medical officer, probation officer, clerical staff, caretakers and service staff.

The superintendent looks after admission procedures of the beneficiaries. The probation officer is the liaison between the beneficiaries and the officials, conducts home visits and handles the networking aspect of the organization. As a government-funded organization it is barred from raising funds on its own. From the funds allocated to the WCD department, Organization C gets approximately 200,000 to 300,000 rupees.

(b) Profile of children cared for

Girls in distress are the institution's target group. Its beneficiaries are mainly from dysfunctional families, sometimes under economic pressure. Some of them are unmarried mothers and they may have been exploited in the sex trade. The girls come primarily from Andhra Pradesh, Karnataka, West Bengal and Nepal, and their educational status is very low. Many of the girls are brought in by the police, but they also come on their own if they feel the need for protection. Since it is a government agency people are aware of it and the girls do not find it difficult to get information about it. The age group served is from infancy to 18. The institution does not encourage the girls to stay on indefinitely, but in cases in which a girl does not have any other support system, the length of her stay is extended. Since this organization is a recent addition to the WCD department, this home was housing only 14 girls at the time of data collection. At the time of writing this report, there were 45 girls.

(c) Personnel

Professionals who are perceived to have an attitude of genuineness towards work with children make up the organization. There are twelve workers in total, all of them paid, with the exception of the medical officer who receives an honorarium. The pay scale of this organization was not revealed. For the post of probation officer they employ people with Masters in Social Work degrees, but for the rest, including the superintendent's post, there are no specific qualifications. Ironically, the probation officer, with a master's degree, has to report to the superintendent, who currently is a graduate with no special training. The organization has not placed much emphasis on quality training. A provident fund, gratuities and housing facilities are the benefits the staff receives. The only motivating factor is perceived to be job security.

(d) Services provided

The organization aims to provide shelter to girls rescued from sexual exploitation and to arrange for their reintegration into society. This often involves tracking down their families and helping the girls to rejoin them, but not without the girls' consent. Traditional income-generating skills such as tailoring are taught to all the girls irrespective of individual aptitude and interests. Health care, as explained in the section on comprehensive health problems and counselling, is an important service offered.

50

(e) Achievements, constraints and future plans

The staff of the institution consider their role in the mass raids of brothels in 1996 as a phenomenal achievement. The probation officer who worked with these girls personally accompanied the Nepalese girls to Kathmandu to reintegrate them into their families. This home is now accepting girls rescued from the brothels as a follow-up action of the judiciary and the state WCD department. The department has also set up a home in a nearby district for girls with HIV/AIDS, which is a major achievement. Their strengths include never denying admission to any girl seeking help and ensuring that those in genuine need of intervention get it in time. The organization is aware of its lack of focus on education and its inability to give attention to the individual interests of the children and youth in its care.

List of References

Child Protection Centre – Nepal, 1994. *A report on girl children at risk – Kathmandu Valley* (Kathmandu, Children At Risk: Network Group).

Child Workers in Nepal (CWIN), 1998. State of the Rights of the Child in Nepal, country report.

National Commission for Women, 1997. *The Velvet Blouse: Sexual Exploitation of the Children* (Government of India).

Pradhan, G., ed., 1993. *Misery Behind the Looms: Child Labourers in the Carpet Factories in Nepal* (Kathmandu, Child Workers in Nepal).

Pradhan, G. 1998. *Commercial Sexual Exploitation of Children in Nepal,* with a special reference to trafficking across the Indo-Nepal border (Nepal, Child Workers in Nepal).

Singh, A.K., 1990. *Devadasi System in Ancient India: a study of temple dancing girls of South India* (New Delhi, H.K. Publishers and Distributors).

United Nations Children's Fund (UNICEF), 1997. A Situational analysis of sex work and trafficking in Nepal with reference to children.